THE POTATO PUFF SURPRISE

TOM FLANAGAN

To my daughter Marley who surprises me every day.

ACKNOWLEDGMENTS

Writing this book was a wonderful trip down memory lane and it would not have been possible without my beautiful and talented wife Kathy, who has forgotten more about the passive voice and prepositional phrases than I will ever know. You read every draft no matter how tired or busy you were and always provided meticulous feedback. Thank you so much.

I'm forever grateful to the Kellys for not only allowing me to write about Joe, but encouraging me to do so. Joe Kelly was a lot of things to a lot of people. He was a grandfather, a father, a husband, a painter, and a connoisseur of Battleship Gray. To me, he was simply, Blue. But above all, he was the Kellys' guiding light.

To my critique group: Mike Charpentier, Meghan Cute, Scott Meerbott, and John Sable. Your honesty and integrity were an inspiration. Thank you.

Thank you to Patrick Caldwell for the amazing cover design. Your artwork truly brought this little book to life. Thank you to Kerrie Flanagan who gave me a crash course on the current state of the publishing industry. That was time well spent. And a very special thanks to my editor, Laura Mahal, who possesses the unique ability to simultaneously educate and encourage. That's a true gift. Thank you.

To the old neighborhood: Shawn and Neal Kelly, Jay and John Reddington, Mike and Paul Charpentier, Scott and Glenn Meerbott, Jim Swindells, Marco Carreira, and all of the neighborhood kids who touched my life and made me the person I am today. Cheers.

Last, but certainly not least, I'd like to thank my family. Without you, these memories would not exist.

PREFACE

Growing up, I spent a lot of time with Shawn and Neal Kelly. They had a basketball hoop and I spent countless hours in their driveway attempting three-pointers and occasionally making a shot or two from downtown. The Kellys also had cable television, which made their house a popular place for sleepover parties. They even had a beach house in New Hampshire, and I spent many summer vacations kayaking, boogie boarding, and roasting marshmallows by the fire with the entire family. As a young adult, I had the unique opportunity to work for their dad, Joe Kelly, who owned a home improvement company. It was an experience I will never forget.

This book was inspired by Joe, who died of cancer in 2017. I set out to write a short story that captured a few of his more entertaining antics. Little did I know that it would turn into a book that would transport me back in time. Back to the old neighborhood. Back to junior high school. And back to Rocky Point Amusement Park. I grew up with an eclectic bunch of characters. People like Paul Charpentier, Jay

Reddington, the Meerbotts, and of course, Joe Kelly. Someone needed to tell their story and I'm honored to do so.

Every story in this book is true. I wrote them how I remember them. Some people may have a slightly different recollection, and that's what makes life interesting. Some of the names have been changed to protect the innocent and the not-so-innocent. However, all of the major characters including Mike and Paul Charpentier, Scott and Glenn Meerbott, and Jay and John Reddington have not been changed.

Enjoy.

PROLOGUE

I was ten years old the first time I saw the T-shirt. It was Saint Patrick's Day 1982. It was a beautiful afternoon. The weather in New England during the spring is unpredictable at best. It's not unusual to encounter all four seasons in the same day. I remember this was not one of those days.

I grew up in Pawtucket, Rhode Island and lived in a blue-collar neighborhood. Our core group of friends was comprised of brothers from hardworking families. The group included Mike and Pauly Charpentier, Shawn and Neal Kelly, Jay and John Reddington, my younger brother Timmy, and me. There were other kids who drifted in and out of our lives, but we were the heart and soul of the neighborhood.

Shawn and Neal had a basketball hoop, which made their house a popular destination. Their dad was a painter and a jack-of-all-trades. He built the hoop by hand and hung it on a tree over the driveway. We decided to take advantage of the unseasonably warm weather and play some pickup basketball. We were in the middle of a game when their Dad pulled up in an old white van. He parked on the side of the house, halfway on the sidewalk and halfway in the street. The van was jam-packed with ladders, tarps, equipment, and other implements of destruction.

Joe Kelly stepped out of the van. He pulled up his white overalls and ordered his crew to break down the equipment. Joe was boisterous and sort of cool, in a Keith Richards kind of way.

He continued to bark orders at the crew. "Clean the damn brushes," he said. "And for Chrissakes watch the damn ladder."

I recall that Joe's crew always smelled funny, like cheap beer and a strange skunky smell that I couldn't quite place. And they always seemed to have a good time regardless of how much their fearless leader screamed at them.

Joe walked around the van and headed towards the basketball court. He stopped underneath the hoop and waved us over. We stalled as long as we could, but it was impossible to ignore the guy. "Shawn. Neal. Guys. Get over here," he said. We dropped the ball and formed a semicircle around him.

"Don't tell your parents," he said.

He lifted his T-shirt from his overalls and stretched it lengthwise, so we could see. There on the front of the emerald green shirt, in big white letters, read the following line, "If you don't like the Irish." With a gleam in his eye, he looked left and then right. Convinced that the coast was clear, he took the bottom one-third of his shirt and flipped it inside out, revealing the T-shirt's punch line, which read in even bigger white letters, "Fuck You."

Joe laughed so hard I thought he was going to piss himself. It was a hearty, almost obnoxious, laugh. Shawn was less amused and looked half irritated, half embarrassed. We politely chuckled, ran back onto the court, and resumed the game.

Joe loved the shirt. He wore it like a badge of honor every St. Paddy's Day. It was his uniform at parades, festivals, and barrooms across the state. And he always delivered the punch line with the same passion as he did that one spring afternoon.

1

LABOR DAY WEEKEND 2017

DENVER, COLORADO

I stumbled out of bed and scanned the room for my phone. A gentle breeze drifted through the open window. My wife, Kathy, was wrapped under a white down blanket and still fast asleep. I rubbed my eyes and realized this was not our bedroom. In fact, this wasn't even our house. By the time I found my phone, it was too late. I had missed the call.

We attended a concert the evening before and spent the night with friends. It was a late night and I was still half asleep. I plopped down on the foot of the bed and checked my messages. There was a voicemail from my mom. Her tone conveyed a sense of urgency, and there was the tiniest crack in her voice when she asked me to return her call as soon as possible.

"Hi Mom. It's Tom. Is everything okay?" I asked.

"Thank you for calling me back," she said. "I wanted to let you know that Blue passed away this morning. I'm sorry.

"Are you still there, Tommy?"

"Yeah, I'm still here," I said. "How are Shawn and Neal doing?"

"I'm not sure," she said. "I'm going to visit in a few minutes."

"Please keep me posted."

"I will. Love you," she said.

"I love you too, Mom."

Kathy rolled over and poked her head out of the soft down blanket that was now half draped over the bed.

"What's up?" she asked.

"Joe Kelly died," I said.

2

RHODE ISLAND

THE BIGGEST LITTLE STATE IN THE UNION

I took out my phone and snapped a photo of the parking lot sign.

"I'm in section two of the economy lot," I said.

I heard a loud engine decompress and begin to rev. I turned around and saw the shuttle bus. It was about twenty yards away and heading towards the passenger pickup station.

"Shit," I said.

I grabbed my suitcase and ran after the bus. The whirlwind continued through Denver International Airport as I navigated my way through security and to the gate.

I boarded the plane, sat back in my seat, and closed my eyes. I gripped the armrest as the plane took off. After a bit of turbulence, which always makes me nervous, I closed my eyes and tried to relax.

It was my first opportunity to process Joe's death. The last time I saw him, I was living in Marin County, outside of San Francisco, and was visiting Rhode Island for the holidays. He had suffered a stroke and was in rehab. Kathy, his wife, was thrust into the role of caregiver. Not an easy task given Joe's disposition.

Joe's walker clattered across the ceramic tile floor as he limped towards the kitchen table. He wore a dark grey fedora that, oddly enough, complimented his long sleeve thermal and blue plaid pajamas. His goatee was now weathered and atrium white.

"Flanagan, hawhyya?" he asked.

I always got a kick out of the way Joe enunciated, "How are you?" Despite his poor health, he sat down at the table and rolled a joint.

"It's good to see you, Blue," I said. "Glad to see some things haven't changed."

"What, this?" he asked. "It's my medicine."

I asked him how he was feeling and how rehab was going. He quickly changed the subject. I glanced at Kathy and she raised an eyebrow. It was clearly a topic he did not want to discuss. I switched gears and turned to Neal.

"I got you a Christmas gift," I said and handed him a bottle of Pliny the Elder, an IPA brewed in Northern California.

"Awesome. Thank you."

"Let's crack it," I said.

Joe was a former homebrewer and appreciated a small taste of the hoppy, West Coast ale.

"Flanagan, when I croak, I want you to read my eulogy."

I was caught off guard and tried to defuse the gravity of the situation with a lame joke.

"You'll outlive all of us, you old goat," I said.

Joe looked me dead in the eye.

"I'm serious, Tom."

I paused for a moment. Joe was a character, a true original. There were dozens of entertaining stories other people could share, but he loved my stories. He took pride in them.

"Of course," I said.

That was the last time I saw Joe Kelly alive. He recovered from the stroke, but was later diagnosed with terminal cancer. He had overcome numerous health issues in the past, and a small piece of me thought he would actually beat it.

After the funeral services, the Kellys would be hosting an Irish wake of sorts at the Galway Bay to celebrate Joe's life. This is where I would deliver his eulogy. The Galway is an Irish pub in the old neighborhood I grew up in. It's a gritty little place that lacks amenities, but certainly not character. It's located behind McCoy Stadium, home of the Pawtucket Red Sox (the Boston Red Sox Triple-A affiliate), and across the street from Jenks Junior High School.

I thought about the Galway and the smell of roasted malt and barley from a freshly poured Guinness. I thought about McCoy Stadium and how the longest game in baseball history was played there. The PawSox beat the Rochester Red Wings in a thirty-three-inning marathon that featured Wade Boggs and Cal Ripken Jr., two future Hall of Famers.

I pictured the spectacular murals of former players painted by Rhode Island School of Design graduate, Tayo Heuser. I imagined the field. The grass and dirt were perfectly manicured. A spectrum of blue, yellow and red cascaded across the infield as a garden hose passed through the shadows. The grounds crew worked methodically, putting the final touches on the field. The tarp was lifted from the pitcher's mound and the bases were inserted into the ground.

I recalled selling popcorn in the stands when I was a kid. Selling popcorn was a good gig. Not only was it the lightest snack to carry up and down the stadium stairs, it also generated the highest profit margin. Unlike soda, which was super heavy and cost a $1.75 a cup, a box of popcorn was only $1.50. Most people gave you $2.00 and let you keep the change. Then I thought about junior high school.

3

JENKS JUNIOR HIGH SCHOOL

PAWTUCKET, RHODE ISLAND

Jenks Junior High School was a melting pot of human physiology encapsulated in a concrete building that was appropriately painted institutional white. Although it was only twenty feet away from Agnes E. Little, the elementary school that I attended, the two schools were worlds apart.

A piece of me missed elementary school. It was predictable. You sat at the same desk, in the same classroom, and had the same teacher for the entire day. This routine was a good fit for my personality. I missed my beloved number two pencils that were engraved with my name. I missed the smell of my Paper Mate Pink Pearl eraser. I missed my trusty Trapper Keeper that organized my homework. But most of all, I missed my Star Wars lunch box. It was a vintage metal lunch box that had numerous scenes from the movie painted on all six sides. It also had a cool thermos with C-3PO and R2-D2 pictured on the front. Unfortunately, these tools of the trade weren't cool in junior high.

In contrast, junior high school had multiple floors. Each subject was held in a different classroom.

There were strange new classes like home economics and

sex education. Homework had to be written with a pen, a requirement that was strictly enforced. And for the first time in my academic career, I was assigned a locker.

The students had changed as well. There were guys with facial hair who spent the day making out with girls who could pass for runway models. There were tattooed criminals from juvenile detention. And of course, there was a bully. Every school has one, and the bully at Jenks Junior High ruled the halls with an iron fist. To this day, I shudder to say her name out loud.

Jenks was a short tour of duty that brought students from numerous school districts together for just two years, who would then part ways and be shuffled off to various high schools across the state. With the exception of Shawn and Neal, whose parents shipped them off to Saint Teresa's, a private Catholic school, our neighborhood gang all went to Jenks Junior High School.

Scott and Glenn Meerbott were one of four sets of twins at school. I swear there was something in the Pawtucket water that spawned this anomaly. They lived a few blocks from our neighborhood and went to Agnes with us. We played a ton of sports together, but the brothers excelled at football. They were a force to be reckoned with and terrorized the playing field. Their signature move was to grab a fistful of cold, wet snow and smash it into your face after a tackle. Scott and Glenn were also ruthless ballbusters and were responsible for the vast majority of nicknames at school. It was their forte. For instance, Mike and Pauly's mom had a penchant for thrift stores and made them wear vintage, secondhand jackets. So, the Meerbotts dubbed Mike and Pauly "Jacket and Coat."

Jay's favorite basketball player was Larry Bird. Naturally, Jay's nickname was "Jay Bird." One day, the twins overheard Mr. Blanchette, my nosy neighbor, reprimanding Timmy. In the heat of battle, Blanchette declared that my brother had a head like a cow. The Meerbotts found this to be the best thing since sliced bread and bestowed upon him the nickname of, "Cowhead." Timmy hated this name.

Jenks Junior High had an interesting mix of teachers, and Mr. Lupo and Mr. Palo were my two favorites. Mr. Lupo taught science and fancied himself as the "cool" teacher. His brother Pat played bass for John Cafferty and The Beaver Brown Band, a popular Rhode Island rock band that hit it big producing the soundtrack for the movie *Eddie and The Cruisers*.

Mr. Palo was the school's music teacher. He made the entire class watch the Woodstock movie. We had to have permission slips signed by our parents in order to watch the film. Only one student did not get permission and had to wait outside the classroom for the duration of the movie. Personally, I enjoyed watching the sex, drugs and rock 'n' roll.

My parents were hippies and had survived the counterculture movement. The Meerbotts joked that it was my parents on the front cover of the Woodstock album. Although the young couple wrapped in the muddy blanket looked like my parents, it was not. However, I took this wisecrack as a compliment.

4

___

THE BULLY

She strutted through the entrance of the eighth grade corridor. Her long, greasy red hair camouflaged her face as she surveyed the hallway. She rolled past the first section of lockers and classroom doors. I heard a grunt, alarmingly close, and looked up.

"Oh God. I think she saw us," I said.

"Nah, it's fine. We're cool," Jay replied.

The tone of Jay's voice provided little comfort. I held the lock with my left hand, made the final rotation of the dial and pulled. Nothing. The sequence must have been off by a hair. My hands began to tremble.

Focus, I said to myself.

I rotated the dial three hundred and sixty degrees and paused at the indicator located above the number zero. I took a deep breath and turned the dial clockwise, then counter-clockwise, then I stopped at the last digit of my combination and pulled down on the lock. Success. I exhaled and open the door.

"She's headed right towards us," Jay stammered.

"Don't make eye contact," I said.

She didn't say a word as she approached our locker section. She tossed Jay aside and, without breaking stride, swept me off my feet. Her large, sweaty hands were clamped under my arms. My black high-top Chuck Taylors dangled in mid-air. I saw the open locker out of the corner of my eye and realized the inevitable. She shoved me into the locker and slammed the door shut. My shoulder caught the edge of the coat hanger and I winced in pain. With the exception of a single ray of light that penetrated through the locker's vent, it was pitch-black inside. The attack happened so fast it almost didn't register.

"Hold on, Flanagan. I'm coming to gettcha," Jay shouted from the outside.

Jay swung the door open, grabbed my hand, and pulled me from the locker. The incident caused a bit of a scene in the hall. A few kids pointed and laughed. Others looked bewildered. I took a moment to compose myself. A sharp pain pierced through my shoulder and I could feel an open cut on my neck. However, the emotional trauma was far worse than any physical pain. I was embarrassed.

Jay Reddington always had my back. We met on the first day of elementary school and became the best of friends. Like many kids, we bonded in the cafeteria, a sacred place where many friendships and alliances are forged. Unbeknownst to the teachers, the cafeteria provided a safe haven that featured a thriving underground economic system based on trade and barter. Jay hated the whole milk that was served at lunch. His mom would pack him a ziplock bag full of Nesquik Chocolate powder every day to transform his milk into a delicious chocolate shake. Jay would split half of his Nesquik with me, and in return, I would share my Hostess Cakes with him.

We both loved *Star Wars*. It was the first movie that I ever saw, and it had a profound impact on my life. I had the action figures, the vehicles, the bedroom set, the Halloween costumes, I even had the underwear. Jay had the Millennium Falcon. It was the holy grail of toys. We spent hours pretending to be Han Solo and flying the Falcon through hyperspace. One day, we were engrossed in an after-school lightsaber battle. The toy weapon came in numerous styles. For instance, my lightsaber glowed in the dark. Dennis, one of the neighborhood kids, had a hollow lightsaber. It made a humming sound when you swung it, similar to the sound in the movies.

I was engaged in a variety of Jedi combat maneuvers. My lightsaber became an extension of my hand as I raced up and down the street eluding Stormtroopers and performing Jedi mind tricks on unsuspecting space aliens. Unfortunately, in my crusade to save the universe, I didn't notice that Dennis had put a stick in his laser sword. He swung the sword right at my face. The stick exploded out of his lightsaber and hit me right in the eye. My legs buckled, and I collapsed to the ground. Blood began to trickle down my face. I covered my eyes with both hands, hoping to simultaneously alleviate the blood that spewed out of my wound and to hide the tears that rolled down my face.

Not only did Jay beat the heck out of Dennis, he ran and got my mom, who rushed me to the emergency room. I had to wear an eye patch for a month. Although, I sort of looked like one of the space bandits from the Mos Eisley spaceport in the original Star Wars movie. So, that was pretty cool.

Jay and I were a team and persevered through elementary school, but junior high was uncharted territory.

5

A DANGEROUS GAME

Classroom etiquette was different in junior high, and there was no shortage of sophomoric hijinks. Zach was the class clown. He was a bit of a loner and didn't have many friends. He wore a Triple F.A.T. Goose jacket every day and sported a rattail haircut. I sat across from Zach in Home Economics class. The topic was, "How to make a Magic Egg." Also known as "Egg-in-a-Hole," "Egg in the basket," or my personal favorite, "The One-Eyed Jack." The process is pretty straightforward and something the class could make at home. You butter a slice of bread, cut a hole in the center, crack the egg into the hole, and cook until golden brown. That's it.

Our teacher was prepping the ingredients and had her back to the class. Like most class clowns, Zach was an opportunist and took full advantage of the situation. He began to break pencils. He grabbed a pencil with his left hand and slid it under his index finger, over his middle finger and under the ring finger of his right hand. He then gripped the pencil and slapped his hand, with authority, over his knee. The pencil exploded like a cluster bomb—propelling jagged splinters in every direction.

Freddie was sitting on the other side of Zach and was hit with the debris.

"Ouch. Cut it out," Freddie said.

"Shut up, dickwad," Zach said.

Jen, who was sitting in the front of the class taking notes, turned around.

"Shh," she hushed.

"It," Zach responded in an instant.

Duping a classmate into saying the word "shit" was one of Zach's favorite pranks, and the gag prompted a few giggles throughout the classroom.

"Hey Jen," Zach said. "Douchebag says what?"

"What?" Jen replied.

Again, he mumbled the first part, "Douchebag says" and overemphasized the second part, "what?"

"Oh, grow up, Zach," Jen said.

Although these shenanigans could be a nuisance, they were harmless, and at times even funny. However, Zach also engaged in another game. One with much higher stakes and serious consequences. He would actively provoke "Her." For instance, he would enunciate sound effects under his breath as she walked down the hall.

"Boom, boom."

"Crunch, crunch."

"Drudge, drudge."

This made her angry. Seeking vengeance, she would stop and scan the corridor for the perpetrator. Some people laughed, but most looked away in fear. This was a dangerous game and I kept my distance throughout the school year.

6

SCHOOL LUNCH

I missed a lot of things about elementary school, but lunch was not one of them. Only one meal a day was served at Agnes E. Little and you were out of luck if you didn't like the daily special. Bringing your lunch from home was the only alternative. This rigid structure produced the trade system. That economy was born out of necessity. Junior high, conversely, was capitalism at its best.

The menu changed daily and featured a plethora of options: pizza, burgers, chicken sandwiches, and more. There were numerous side dishes available as well. However, potato puffs were the crème de la crème. Crispy, deep-fried, golden brown puffs of potato. When prepared with love, potato puffs were a small slice of heaven. Junior high also had the best desserts money could buy. The strawberry shortcake ice cream bars were my favorite and were typically only available in the summertime, from the finest ice cream trucks in town.

I walked into the cafeteria. The lunch line had already formed and began to wrap around the corner. I walked to the end of the line and stepped in behind Freddie.

"What are you getting today?" Freddie asked.

"Potato puffs for sure," I said as the line moved forward.

"I'm in the mood for pizza," Freddie said. "And maybe some chocolate pudding."

I heard a scuffle coming from the back and turned to investigate.

"Oh crap," I said.

"What's the matter?" Freddie asked.

She marched right down the line. I saw her elbow a kid behind us and shove another.

"Here she comes. Don't make eye contact," I said.

"Hey, she's cutting," Freddie said.

"Quiet," I whispered under my breath. "Don't make a move."

She cut right in front of Freddie and staked her claim in the line, which was now close to the front of the kitchen. Freddie, a bit of a stickler, did not appreciate this blatant disregard for the rules. He began to perform exaggerated gestures behind her back. He held his nose with his left hand and fanned with his right, pretending he caught a whiff of some pungent body odor. Then he did something gross with his finger.

I was horrified and tried to look away. My chest began to hurt. I had a flashback of the vicious attack at my locker. Freddie continued to perform a variety of inappropriate gestures. She turned around as he fluttered alongside her in a trancelike state. Clearly not paying attention, he continued to perform. She was not amused and watched Freddie for what seemed like an eternity.

I wanted to scream, *Stop it! Turn around, you fool*, but nothing came out. I was petrified.

She took a step forward and was just inches from Freddie. He finally looked up, but it was too late. She grabbed Freddie's face with her enormous right hand and rammed the back of his head into the concrete wall that encapsulated the school cafeteria. The strike was calculated and extremely potent. He was knocked unconscious and slid straight down to the floor. To this day, I'll never forget the look of despair on Freddie's face the moment before the attack.

I stood there frozen, trying make sense of what just happened. I prayed that she wouldn't find me guilty by association. As luck would have it, she turned around and focused her attention on another student.

Thank God, I thought, as I exhaled a sigh of relief.

She walked up to the kid and snatched his brownie off the tray. There wasn't anything the poor kid could do except grin and bear it. A classmate helped Freddie to his feet and another student actually left the line to find a teacher.

Jay and the Meerbotts had already grabbed a table and were sitting down. I rushed over and pulled up a seat.

"Holy crap," I said. "Did you guys see that?"

"No, what happened?" Jay asked.

"You're not going to believe this one," I said and provided a play-by-play analysis of what just transpired.

"Is he still alive?" Jay asked half-jokingly. Everyone at the table laughed.

"She also stole another kid's brownie," I said.

This revelation brought the laughter to a halt and raised a couple of eyebrows. The school brownies had a mysterious reputation. Legend had it that a kid once traded for a bunch of the brownies, scraped off all of the nuts and compiled them into a super tight ball. The nuts became unstable and ignited, causing a small explosion in the cafeteria. I was never able to confirm the validity of the "nut bomb," but the story seemed plausible to me.

Bobby walked over and sat down at the table. He lived

down the street from the Meerbotts and was one of the pickiest eaters I had ever met. We all did a double take when he put down his tray. The cafeteria trays were well designed and featured surprisingly thoughtful usability. They were divided into compartments that were designed to accommodate an entrée, a side, dessert, and a small carton of milk. However, every compartment in Bobby's tray was filled with chocolate pudding.

"Not again," I said.

He had done the exact same thing just last week. The Meerbotts were in rare form, delivering zinger after zinger. The table roared with laughter as the twins crafted joke after joke. At one point, Bobby laughed so hard that pudding shot straight out of his nose. This became an instant classic and solidified the Meerbotts as comedic geniuses.

Everyone at the table took one look at his tray and had the exact same thought. We began to belittle each other with a variety of tasteless jokes in an attempt to spark another chocolate pudding snot rocket.

"You smell like cat piss, Flanagan."

I grew up in a house full of pets and these types of one-liners always struck a nerve with me.

"Screw you," I said.

Jay covered his face with the palm of his hand and cracked a joke about Scott's appearance. Scott countered with, "If I had a face like that, I'd cover it too."

Of course, there was no shortage of unoriginal "Yo Momma" jokes.

Unfortunately, Bobby demonstrated a great deal of constraint and kept a stiff upper lip. With no repeat performance in sight, the comedy roast was losing steam. I saw this as an opportunity and plotted my exit.

"I'm going to hit the restroom before my next class," I said.

"Okay. I'll catch up with you later," Jay replied.

7

DIARRHEA OF A MADMAN

I saw a large poster taped to the door as I walked towards the exit of the cafeteria. The headline read, "Homecoming Dance —Friday Night." However, it was the subheading, "Featuring DJ Luke," that caught my attention. Luke was the owner of Luke's Record Exchange on Broadway in Pawtucket.

The tiny store was jam-packed with vinyl records and cassette tapes. Posters, tapestries, and colorful tie-dyes were plastered throughout the shop. The place was a stomping ground for bikers, rappers, metalheads, old hippies, and other eclectic characters.

The PA system went to eleven and would have made Spinal Tap guitarist, Nigel Tufnel, proud. The Rolling Stones were always in heavy rotation. Luke was the ultimate hustler. He'd be knee-deep in a pile of old Beatles albums as he wheeled and dealed with customers. The scene was reminiscent of Shakedown Street at a Grateful Dead concert.

Mike and I were regulars. We spent hours in the store in search of vintage KISS memorabilia, hoping to find a sealed copy of *Love Gun* or the special KISS comic book that was printed with the band's actual blood.

My Christmas list included a few albums the previous year, and "*Diary of a Madman*" by Ozzy Osborne was at the top of the list. The cover artwork was beyond cool. Ozzy is standing in what appears to be a library, inside a creepy castle that is covered in cobwebs. An assortment of candles illuminates the scene. There is a young boy, maybe five or six years old, sitting behind an altar with a mischievous grin. He is reading from a book of spells. Behind the boy is a bookcase with a human skull resting on the shelf. Ozzy's outfit is torn to shreds and he is covered in blood. He looks deranged. The title is located at the bottom of the album and is written in a large, comic book style font that pops off the cover. I had to have it.

I was ecstatic when I found it under the tree. My mom told me that she was embarrassed when she purchased it at Luke's.

"Mom, it's just a heavy metal album," I said.

Apparently, my mom had walked into Luke's Record Exchange, couldn't read my handwriting, and asked if they had "Diarrhea" of a Madman. The cashier blushed and asked if my mom had meant, "Diary of a Madman." Bewildered, my mom purchased the cassette and dashed out of the store.

This dance could be fun, I thought.

It was the last period of the day and I had hit the wall. I was zoned out and had been staring at the clock for the last thirty minutes.

"Finally," I said as the clock struck 2:10 p.m. and the dismissal bell rang.

I bolted out of my seat and rushed over to my locker to meet up with Jay. I grabbed my sweatshirt and a few books, then headed out of the building. We were walking up South Bend Street towards Saint Joseph's Church when I remembered seeing the poster for the Homecoming dance.

"Hey, what are you doing Friday night?" I asked.

"Nothing. What's up?"

"Guess who's DJ'ing the Homecoming dance?" I asked.

"Luke," Jay said. "I saw the poster too. We should go."

"I'm down," I said.

Then we both blurted out at the same time, "We should wear our hats!"

"Pinch, poke, owe me a Coke," I said.

Jay laughed as we cut through the church parking lot.

"See you tomorrow," Jay said.

"Word," I replied.

I hopped up the three cement steps that led to my front door. I unzipped my sweatshirt and fished out the house key that was strung around my neck. I opened the door, walked into the living room, and turned on the TV. I started to hum the intro song to *Scooby-Doo* as I flipped through the channels.

"Scooby Dooby Doo, where are you?"

I found that watching cartoons after a long day of school was the perfect way to unwind. Unfortunately, the television reception was terrible.

My father is an accomplished contrarian. He has always been on the cutting edge of audiovisual equipment. He was an early adopter of video game consoles, the VCR, video cameras, and other home technologies. However, he refused to believe that anyone would pay to watch television. I had to sleep over at Shawn and Neal's house just to watch MTV. In fact, my family was one of the last households in the state to purchase cable TV.

As cable continued to experience unprecedented growth and adoption, my father experimented with obscure set-top box devices like Preview. Preview was a subscription-based service that played a few movies on a loop over a single channel. He also dabbled in military-esque antennas that he constructed on the top of the roof. The antennas were controlled by a rotator system that sat on the top of the television set.

The control unit was about the size of an Atari 2600 and had a large dial in the center of the console. I turned the dial back and forth for a few minutes until I heard an ominous clicking sound on the roof. I gave up and turned on PBS, one of the few channels with decent reception. *The Joy of Painting* with Bob Ross had just started. Van Dyke Brown, Titanium White, Prussian Blue and Midnight Black animated across the bottom of the screen. I was mesmerized as Bob blended colors and worked his way across the canvas.

"Beat the devil out of it, Bob," I said as he began to clean his brush.

"Tommy, it's time to get ready for dinner," my mom called out from the kitchen.

"What are we having?" I asked.

"Shepherd's pie," she said.

"Coming!"

8

THE HOMECOMING DANCE

Jay and I walked through the cafeteria doors and into the dance as Nena sang about ninety-nine luftballons. We were both wearing thin white slacks, pastel T-shirts, no socks, and our brand-new Panama hats.

Mike Charpentier took one look at us and burst out laughing.

"Who invited Crockett and Tubbs?" he asked.

We were oblivious to his next *Miami Vice* joke and walked right by him.

"Let's check out the scene," Jay said.

The cafeteria had been transformed into a dance hall. There was a large "Homecoming Dance" banner mounted to the wall at the far end of the cafeteria, and party streamers were draped throughout. The DJ booth was located under the banner. Luke's turntables were surrounded by a row of speakers.

A row of nerds and wallflowers were planted along the left side of the cafeteria. I glanced over and saw a kid trip on his untied shoelace and stumble into a classmate. A few others were caught up in nervous chitchat. I saw another kid in the back who appeared to be engaged in a serious game of Pocket Pool. These were my people, but I suspected these kids may have been coerced by their parents to attend the event. The right side of the cafeteria was a smorgasbord of hedonism as cool, young couples were immersed in make out sessions. Serious make out sessions.

A circle began to form in the center of the cafeteria as "99 Luftballoons" gave way to a thunderous bass line and the song transitioned to "Jam on It" by Newcleus.

"Whoa, breakdancing," Jay said.

"Let's go watch," I said.

The battle was in full swing by the time Jay and I reached the circle. We squeezed our way in to get a better look. There was kid in the center of the circle who spun around on the palm of his hand. His body was about twelve inches off the ground. His elbow was tucked under his belly and his right hand supported his entire body. He spun faster and faster, then stopped on a dime. The crowd roared with approval. I always admired the athleticism of breakdancing. A few more kids joined in. They exchanged an array of dazzling maneuvers that included back spins, head spins, and windmills.

Unfortunately, Cosmo D and the breakdancing came to an abrupt end when Luke switched gears and broke into Madonna's "Crazy for You." This prompted the entire right side of the cafeteria onto the dance floor as the breakdancing circle morphed into a sea of slow dancing.

"Flanagan, check that out. That dude has both of his hands stuffed into that chick's back pockets."

"That he does," I said as I tried to pretend that I wasn't impressed or even a bit jealous.

"Leave it to Madonna," Jay said.

We navigated our way through the sea of horny teenagers and headed to the sidelines to hang out with some classmates.

Luke wove a musical tapestry that delighted students and teachers throughout the evening.

As the dance was winding down, Luke got on the mic and announced the last song of the night. Jimmy Page plucked the opening notes to "Stairway to Heaven," which prompted a mad dash to the dance floor. Couples jockeyed for position, trying to find a sliver of privacy. Jay bumped into a girl he knew and asked her to dance.

Impressive. Most impressive, I thought.

There are unwritten rules at a school dance. The most significant of these rules is that the DJ will always play "Stairway to Heaven" as the final song of the night. Coming in at eight minutes and two seconds, this power ballad is a force to be reckoned with. It has everything: acoustic guitars, woodwind instruments, cryptic lyrics, mystical vocals, thunderous drums, and an epic electric guitar solo. The song could make or break relationships.

Not to be outdone, I turned to the girl who was hanging out with our little group. She wasn't in any of my classes and I barely knew her. She was also out of my league. Way out of my league. I took a deep breath, then swallowed.

"Do you want to dance?" I asked as I looked down at the floor, too nervous to make eye contact.

"Sure," she said.

I couldn't believe she agreed to dance with me. My body tingled. The palms of my hands began to sweat. I was overcome with joy. Luke continued to talk over the intro of the song.

"We have a dedication," he announced. "This one's going out to Tommy Flanagan." He paused for a moment. "And Tammy Lee Johansson."

Did he just say what I thought he said? The feeling of joy was instantly extinguished and replaced with anxiety, fear, and discombobulation. I looked towards the far end of the cafeteria and saw Mike Charpentier standing next to the DJ booth. Grinning from ear to ear, he nodded his head and pointed at me. A chill ran down my spine.

"What have you done, Mike?"

I turned and looked to my left. She was about twenty feet away. We made eye contact.

Oh crap, I thought.

I could feel her anger from across the room. Her pimpled cheeks flared as red as her hair. She squinted as the left corner of her upper lip rose to her nostril and revealed the most ominous smirk I have ever seen. She punched her right fist into the open palm of her left hand. The crack of her knuckles shattered the delicate sound of Jimmy Page's acoustic guitar.

Without hesitation, I made a beeline for the exit. I ran as fast as I could, but she was able to close the gap. I could feel her breath on the back of my neck as we exited the cafeteria and headed down the hall in the opposite direction of the teachers. My new Panama hat flew off my head. A combination of sweat and tears began to run down my face and blur my vision. I felt a faint tug on the back of my shirt.

It's over. She's got me, I thought.

Her grunts grew louder and more sinister. This was a fight-or-flight situation and unfortunately, there was no way I would survive the fight. I contemplated a tuck and roll maneuver that would allow me to switch direction, but it was too dangerous at this speed. I felt a sharp pain under my rib cage and was beginning to cramp.

I saw a brown door with a silver, horizontal push bar at the end of the hall and prayed that it was unlocked. I lunged forward and threw my entire body into the door. It flew open and I stumbled outside into the crisp autumn air. I sensed a bit of separation, but she was still on my heels.

She's like The Terminator.

We ran stride for stride across the basketball court. I could see the crosswalk at the corner of Johnson Street and South Bend as we headed towards the tennis court. Then something magical happened. Her grunts began to dissipate, and she began to gasp for air. I turned my head slightly over my left shoulder and looked behind me. She was pulling up; she was actually pulling up. I couldn't believe it.

"It's a miracle!" I cried.

My second wind kicked in as I was about to climb the stairs that led to the street. I could see from my peripheral vision that she was bent over with the palms of her hands rested on her knees as she tried to catch her breath. She then turned and began to walk back in the direction of the school. I ran all the way home and never looked back.

Junior high school was an awkward bridge to cross. It was strange, beautiful, and at times, pretty darn scary. One minute you're about to dance with a cute girl, the next you're running for your life. When I look back, it was only two years, but goddamn, it was an experience I'll never forget.

"May you build a ladder to the stars. And climb on every rung. May you stay forever young."

-Bob Dylan

9

THE FUNERAL

"Please make sure your seat backs and tray tables are in their full upright position," the flight attendant announced.

I lost my breath for a fraction of a second. I opened my eyes and tried to focus. I reached for the armrest. My muscles twitched as I pulled myself up in the seat. I had drifted off to sleep and the announcement startled me.

A flight attendant rushed past my row as she stuffed empty plastic cups into a light blue trash bag. The other crew members prepared the cabin for landing as the aircraft made its final approach towards Logan International Airport.

"Ladies and gentlemen, welcome to Boston," the captain announced.

It was a smooth, uneventful landing. I once read that the best way to thank a pilot is to compliment the landing and I make it a point to do so after every flight. I exited the plane and headed towards the passenger pick-up level to meet James, my brother-in-law. It was a long night, and I crashed as soon we got back to his place in Pawtucket.

The next day, I met my mother, father, Timmy and my sister Kate at the William Tripp Funeral Home on Newport

Avenue. I was handed a small white button that read, "I Love Pawtucket." I pinned it to my jacket. The button was a nice touch and complimented my suit, which I deliberately crafted as a subtle tribute to Joe. I wore a powder blue dress shirt and a psychedelic Jerry Garcia tie.

Joe gave me my first Grateful Dead album when I was thirteen years old. It was the iconic "Skull and Roses" live album from 1971. Like many kids my age, I grew up on the Beatles, the Stones, and the Who. However, I had never heard anything like the Dead before. In fact, I felt like I was in possession of something pornographic. I hid the album under my bed for some time. Joe had lived on Haight-Ashbury in San Francisco for a bit and told me a story about the Summer of Love when he handed me the record. Although his sly, half smile gave me the impression he wasn't telling the whole story.

I took a few minutes to catch up with my family and express my condolences to the Kellys. Then I met with the other pallbearers to address the details of our responsibilities.

The sound of a bagpipe echoed off the facade of Saint Teresa's Church as family and friends shuffled across the lawn and up the stairs to the entrance. The bagpipe is a haunting instrument. In certain situations, a single note can conjure up a spectrum of emotions. This was one of those situations.

I focused on the positive as we carried the casket into the church, down the center aisle, and towards the chancel. I reflected on the time Joe and I spent together. I thought about the Kellys' annual Christmas Eve party and the familiar laughter of old friends. The warmth of the fire. The smell of pepperoni, crackers, and cheese plates. "Into the Mystic" by Van Morrison began to play in my head.

"I wanna rock your gypsy soul. Just like way back in the

days of old. Then magnificently we will float into the mystic."

Those were good times.

The church was beautiful. The mid-morning September sun pierced through the stained glass windows and saturated the altar with a kaleidoscope of colors. I sat back in the hard, wooden pew. It was a traditional Roman Catholic service and in a blink of an eye, it was over.

10

THE GALWAY BAY

I gazed out of the window from the back seat of Timmy's pickup truck as we drove down Columbus Avenue. A mix of single-family homes and apartments lined the street on both sides. I had not been on this side of town in a few years. The cracked pavement and uneven sidewalks made the neighborhoods appear weathered and run-down. We passed the homes of friends and local businesses. We drove by Joe's old storage facility, which was converted into a small, street level apartment and no longer stored ladders and paint buckets. The fire station was on the right and the Mei King Chinese restaurant was across the street. We passed the Right Spot, a cozy family-owned diner that specializes in New York System wieners. Despite the name, New York System wieners are a Rhode Island delicacy.

To the untrained eye of a tourist, a hot wiener may resemble the typical hot dog that you would have at a baseball game or Fourth of July cookout. However, a wiener is made from a combination of pork and veal and tastes quite different. It is topped with mustard, onions and a secret meat sauce. Although, I prefer mine with no onions.

The giant wooden shamrock attached to the front entrance glistened in the sun as we pulled into the parking lot of the Galway. "Céad Míle Fáilte" is engraved into the shamrock. The phrase is an Irish greeting that means, "A hundred thousand welcomes." The pub has hosted numerous family events for us including my Aunt Pat's Seventy-fifth birthday party and my parents' 40th wedding anniversary. I've always appreciated the Galway's hospitality.

A guitar player sat at the front of the bar. The smell of distilled Irish whiskey began to fill the air as the sound of an acoustic guitar inundated the small pub. Jay was unable to make the trip back home. However, his mother Sherry, who I hadn't seen in several years, attended the funeral and the celebration. Pauly and his mom stopped by. Even Scott Meerbott came out to toast Joe one last time. Scott and I reminisced about junior high school. Before I knew it, the Galway was jam-packed and it was time to read the eulogy.

I'm not going to lie; it was a challenge to write. I mean, how do you articulate a person's entire life in a twenty-minute speech? Joe was crass and had a zest for life. I wanted to talk about how proud he was of his Irish heritage and how he would wear a funny T-shirt every Saint Patrick's Day. I wanted people to know that he taught me about craftsmanship and how I worked for his home improvement company for a couple of summers when I was a young adult. And I wanted to discuss his love for the blues. So, I tried to tell a story that captured all of those things.

"The blues ain't about feeling better, it's about making other people feel worse."

-Bleeding Gums Murphy

11

THE BLUE MAN

A ROMANCE IN BATTLESHIP GRAY

Joe handed Jay and I two beat-up scrapers, two 3-inch poly-ester blended paintbrushes, and a gallon of Battleship Gray. Battleship Gray was the old man's signature color and he bestowed it liberally, painting doors, foundations, shutters, and even picnic tables. It was our first day on the job and our assignment was to paint his front porch.

"Okay you two, here's the deal. I want you to scrape the entire porch. Then I want you to caulk and seal any holes. After that, you can prime and paint it."

"Any questions?" he asked.

"Do you have any gloves?" I asked.

He seemed to look right through me. His eyes rolled in disgust, and his thick, brown mustache tilted to one side. He straightened the brim of his white cotton painter's cap and turned to Jay.

"Don't forget to use a drop cloth," he said. "I don't want to find a single paint chip on the front lawn. Got it?"

"Got it," Jay said.

Joe walked over to his blue cargo van that was parked

halfway on the sidewalk and halfway in the street and slammed the van's sliding door shut.

"I'll be back in a few hours. Don't fuck anything up," he said as he jumped into the van and drove off.

Joe was an ex-hippie from the 1960s and had the record collection to prove it. Dylan, the Dead, Jefferson Airplane, Quicksilver Messenger Service, Country Joe and the Fish, Hendrix—he had it all. He went to Woodstock and was pretty proud of it. He even saved his sleeping bag from the legendary three-day hippie festival. He stored it, amongst other things, in his basement. I once asked him if he took the infamous brown acid. He looked me dead in the eye.

"Flanagan, I took the brown, the blue, the green, and any other color that came my way."

Joe was a product of the counterculture. He embraced the idealism of the 1960s, particularly the methodology of expanding one's consciousness. However, his true love was the blues. Shawn had a custom T-shirt designed for him as a Christmas gift one year. The shirt had a large photograph of Joe on the front with a slogan that read in a bold, gothic font, "I have a Bluesy Ass."

He adored the shirt. Over the years, his nickname took on a life of its own and saw numerous variations. There was Bluesy Ass, Bluesy, Blue Man, Blue and the more obscure fan favorite, The Blue Shadow. Any given radio station became Joe's lecture hall and an opportunity for him to educate us on the history of the blues. He discussed Robert Johnson and the inner workings of Muddy Waters, Howlin' Wolf and Stevie Ray Vaughan. He taught us about the twelve-bar blues and walking bass lines. It was also an opportunity for Joe to explain to "us kids" why our music sucked.

"This is gonna be a piece of cake, Flanagan."

"Yeah, not a bad way to ease into the summer job," I said.

"We need some tunes," Jay said.

"94 HJY," we declared. Jay and I paused for a moment and looked at each other.

"The Home of Rock 'n' Roll," we both said at the same time.

"Pinch, poke, owe me a Coke," I said.

Jay smiled as we arranged the drop cloth as Joe instructed. It was a heavy-duty drop cloth that was covered in a rainbow of dried paint splatter. I made a mental note of the gratuitous globs of Battleship Gray that were drizzled across the canvas. We covered the front steps, the bushes, and both sides of the porch.

We discovered that home improvement was far more enjoyable if we categorized tasks by songs. We had scraping songs, caulking songs, priming songs, and painting songs. For instance, the steady bass line and primal backbeat of Led Zeppelin's "Whole Lotta Love" was a scraping song. By the same token, "When I Paint My Masterpiece" by Bob Dylan was the perfect painting song.

This methodology could revolutionize the industry, I thought.

Jay and I finished the prep work and were ready to paint. We started at the front of the porch and worked our way back towards the house. We worked with purpose. The paintbrush became an extension of my hand. I felt like a kid swinging a lightsaber again. "For Those About to Rock (We Salute You)" by AC/DC blared from the radio.

"Fire," Brian Johnson, the band's lead singer screamed.

A massive explosion roared from the speakers. Cannons were a staple at the group's live performances, and the sound of the explosion reminded me of an M-80. I turned around and glanced across the street towards Jay's house.

* * *

Jay grew up across the street from the Kellys in a multifamily home. His grandparents lived on the first floor, his aunt and uncle on the second, and Jay and his family occupied the third.

We spent a lot of time at Jay's house. When we were kids, we imagined the backyard was a colosseum. There were epic steel cage matches and battle royals. Championship titles were won, lost, and sometimes even stolen. We transformed his living room into an arena rock show. The stage rotated three hundred and sixty degrees and featured a light show that rivaled Pink Floyd's. The concerts were legendary. We perfected a variety of stage maneuvers that included guitar spins, windmill strums, and drumstick twirls as we lip-synced to Mötley Crüe and Bruce Springsteen. As we grew older, we converted his basement into a rehearsal studio and attempted to play real instruments. We even hosted our first party with actual girls at the house.

But above all, it was our safe house and where we stored illegal contraband. Every summer, Jay's uncles would arm us with enough firepower to take down a small nation. We had bricks of salutes, jumping jacks, Roman candles, and of course, bottle rockets.

Rumor had it that the M-80 was a quarter-stick of dynamite. We heard all kinds of tall tales over the years about kids blowing up everything from mailboxes to above ground swimming pools. However, we had never seen one in person. To us, the M-80 was just an urban legend.

I was at home playing Atari one afternoon. I steadied the joystick and tiptoed towards the edge of the water. I paused for a moment to analyze the timing. I took a step back. The mouths of the three crocodiles closed in unison. I lunged forward and landed on the head of the first beast. I had to act fast and contemplated my second jump. The phone rang.

"Mom, can you get that? I'm in the middle of a game of Pitfall!

I got no response, and the distraction caused me to slip and fall to my death.

"Dammit," I said and ran to the phone.

"Hello."

"Flanagan, get your ass over here," Jay said.

"What's up?" I asked.

"Oh, you'll see. Get over here as fast as possible."

I hung up the phone, rushed outside, and grabbed my bike. I had a sweet Thunder Road Huffy. It was like riding a dirt bike. It had thick, knobby tires and a cool racing plate. I jumped onto the oversized banana seat and peddled as fast as I could.

I made it to Jay's house in record time. I ran up the three flights of stairs and headed into his bedroom.

"This better be good," I said as I tried to catch my breath.

Jay and his brother John were standing in front of the bed with their backs to the bedroom door. Jay turned around. He had a two-inch red tube in his hand. I did a double take. Upon closer inspection, I noticed there was a fuse attached to the center of the tube.

"Is that what I think it is?" I asked.

Jay grinned. "Damn straight it is," he said with a twinkle in his eye. "My uncle gave it to me."

"Holy shit," I said. "Can I see it?" I reached out my hand.

"You see with your eyes not your hands, Flanagan," Jay said.

"C'mon, let me hold it."

Jay handed me the M-80. It was much heavier than I thought it would be.

"It has five grams of flash powder," Jay said.

I looked at John and he nodded.

"When can we light it?" I asked.

There was a moment of silence. Then John looked at Jay. Jay looked at me. And we all smiled.

After a bit of brainstorming, we concocted a simple plan. Jay would light the M-80 and toss it out the bedroom window and into the front yard below.

What could go wrong? I asked myself.

We moved to the other side of the bed and huddled in front of the window, which was about four feet away. Jay reached into his pocket and pulled out a lighter. No words were spoken. Jay flicked the lighter and lifted the flame towards the M-80. The fuse ignited and illuminated in his hand. John and I both took a step back. My right arm twitched as the hair on the back of my neck stood up. A billow of grey smoke drifted out the window and the smell of burning wax began to spread across the room. I locked eyes with Jay.

Throw the damn thing, I thought.

He hesitated for a moment, turned his head towards the window, and tossed the firecracker. It floated through the air in slow motion. The three of us leaned forward and followed its trajectory. I was about to take a step forward, then it happened. The M-80 hit the windowsill and ricocheted back into the room.

We watched in horror as it bounced off the wall, skittered across the floor, and finally came to a stop. Unfortunately, the only course of action was to take cover. Jay bolted towards the foot of the bed. John wedged himself at the side of the headboard. And I jumped over the bed. I landed on my belly, covered my ears, and tried to wiggle further under the bed. I could see the M-80 on the other side of the room. There was a flash of fire followed by a massive explosion that sent a violent wave across the room. The explosion rocked the house. A picture was knocked off the bureau. Posters were ripped from the wall. The room filled with smoke. My body trembled against the floor. A high-pitched ringing echoed in my ears. I was stunned. I saw Jay as the smoke began to dissipate. He looked dumbfounded as he surveyed the room for damage. John didn't move at all. Then came the aftershock as Jay's mom burst into the room. In all my years, I have never seen Sherry that pissed off.

"What the hell was that?

"What were you thinking?

"Do you know how dangerous that was?"

We had no answers or even a reasonable explanation for our behavior. The smoke cleared, and despite some burnt carpet, there was surprisingly little damage. However, our reign of terror with illicit fireworks was over. Years later, I learned that the M-80 is not a quarter-stick of dynamite, but it certainly lived up to its reputation.

The sound of the next AC/DC explosion stopped me dead in my tracks.

"Oh shit," I said.

Jay and I stood in the middle of the patio, surrounded by wet paint on all sides. We were trapped.

"What do we do now?" I asked.

"Wait for the paint to dry," Jay said as he scratched his head, "Joe won't be home for a couple of hours. Don't worry. No one will be the wiser."

A split second later, Joe's van turned the corner onto Armistice Boulevard.

"Oh fuck," Jay said.

Joe slammed on the brakes as he approached the house. You could hear the equipment in the back of the cargo van crash into the front. The ladders that were strapped to the roof propelled forward about two feet and dangled over the hood of the van. The unmistakable smell of burnt rubber filled the air. I stared into the driver's side window.

Joe's face was beet red. I could see a vein twitching in his forehead, and he began to curse a blue streak. He was about to blow a gasket.

12

JOE'S DOG HOUSE

Jay and I were in Joe's doghouse. The next month of work was tortuous. Joe was determined to teach us discipline and responsibility. We did all of the dirty work and heavy lifting. We clashed with forty-foot ladders. We were overexposed to paint thinner and other occupational hazards. We even battled insects and rodents that had taken up residence in and around the property. Joe, on the other hand, was in charge of coffee runs. His trips to Dunkin' Donuts would take hours, and more often than not, he would return with the wrong orders. Jay and I were left hungry, dehydrated, and sunburned on more than one occasion.

A rumor circulated around the job site that Joe went home to watch pornography while Jay and I were forced to clean up construction debris with our bare hands. I believed the gossip. We were around ten years old when we discovered Joe's collection of dirty magazines hidden away in the basement. He had an appetite for such material.

I also recalled how Joe berated his crew when I was a child. Now, I knew how they must have felt. I was in home improvement hell.

13

THE KILLER BEES

We arrived at a new job in Rumford, a small Rhode Island town that borders Southeastern Massachusetts. I was responsible for the shutters, which needed to be scraped, sanded, primed, and painted. I was forever scraping. Jay fired up the radio, a fundamental task in the home improvement industry. He put on 95.5 WBRU, a local college radio station that played modern rock. "Where is my Mind?" by the Pixies came on.

"Jesus Christ that's terrible," Joe said as he changed the station. He turned the dial to public radio and an old blues tune came on. "Now, that's more like it," he said.

The edgy guitar notes and avant-garde lyrics of the Pixies were too much for the old man. Jay and I shook our heads and went to work. I footed the ladder and gave it a couple of firm tugs to confirm its stability. Then I glanced up into the bright sun, squinted, and began my ascent to the second story of the house. My steps were slow and deliberate. I reached the top of the ladder, took out a Phillips-head screwdriver and began to unscrew the shutter. I removed two of the four screws, which created separation between the shutter and the house.

I put the two screws in my back pocket and all of a sudden, I felt a razor-sharp pain on the back my neck, as if a needle had pricked me. Then came a second prick. I winced in pain and felt a heightened sense of anxiety from the undetermined source of the sting. I turned the shutter, a move that I would regret in a matter of seconds. There was a bee nest on the other side. I was ambushed. The onslaught happened in the blink of an eye and the attack was relentless. I ran halfway down the ladder. Overcome by the pain, I jumped.

It was approximately a ten-foot drop, but it felt like twenty. My arms and legs flailed all the way down. I crashed to the ground. The fall knocked the wind out of me. Before I could even catch my breath, I began to roll around the ground hoping to deter the bees. Jay sprinted over.

"Holy shit," he said.

The bees had proven their point and the assault began to dissipate. Joe heard the commotion and walked over to investigate.

"Oh my God. Flanagan, you broke the damn shutter," he said.

During my death-defying leap to safety, the shutter became unhinged, fell to the ground and broke.

"That's coming out of your damn paycheck, Flanagan," Joe said.

"You can't be serious?" I asked. I could have been killed, and this guy was only concerned about a cracked shutter.

"C'mon Flanagan. Let me help you put some mud on those stings," Jay said.

As I stood there covered in mud, extracting stingers from my swollen, red skin, I contemplated my next move.

Revenge is a dish best served cold, Bluesy Ass.

14

GOD'S COUNTRY

I somehow managed to survive the week. My skin was still irritated from the run-in with the bees, my hands were blistered, and my entire body ached. It was payday. I walked over to Joe's to pick up my paycheck before he left to spend the weekend in New Hampshire. He had taken the afternoon off to get ready for the trip, but his van was parked on the street and still had the ladders strapped to the roof when I arrived.

I hope he doesn't make me break the van down, I thought to myself as I labored up the front steps. I could see that the front door was ajar as I stepped onto the porch. I tapped on the door.

"Anyone home?" I asked. Nothing. I knocked again, this time a little harder. "Are you in there, Blue?" Again, I got no response. Something didn't seem right.

I took a peek in and I could smell something burning. I pushed the door open and saw that the stove was engulfed in smoke. I ran over and discovered three fried eggs burning in a pan.

What the heck? I thought.

I turned the burner off, found an oven mitt on the counter,

grabbed the pan and placed it on the back burner. I happened to glance up and see a smoke detector. I was shocked the alarm wasn't triggered. I put the stove's fan on to alleviate the smoke. Did someone tamper with it? Was there an intruder in the house? My imagination began to run wild.

"Hello," I said. "Is anyone home?"

"Flanagan," a voice called out.

I jumped and turned around. I couldn't believe my eyes. Joe appeared in front of his bedroom door. I did a double take. He was completely naked. His hairy, corpulent body cast a shadow across the kitchen.

"My God. Put some damn clothes on, Bluesy," I said.

He was higher than a kite. "Flanagan, you're not going to believe it. I took a magic mushroom, sat down on the bed, and started to watch an old pirate movie on cable. Next thing I know, I thought I was a pirate. It was the damnedest thing," he said.

"Why were there eggs cooking on the stove and more importantly, why the hell are you naked?" I asked.

"What eggs?" he asked.

Good grief. This guy was a piece of work and more irresponsible than Jay and me combined.

The Kellys had a beach house in Rye, New Hampshire, a quaint New England town with a beautiful coastline. It was a cozy little cottage just steps from the beach. The house was built in 1930 and always needed a bit of love. Joe remodeled the kitchen, added a rooftop deck, and even built an outdoor shower made out of driftwood that he collected from the beach. After the two coats of Battleship Gray had dried, Shawn and Neal's Aunt Mary, who was in her eighties at the time, came outside to admire his handy work.

"Mary, take off your clothes and jump in the shower," Joe said.

The mere mention of Mary disrobing outside brought Neal and me to tears and still does to this day.

Of course, Joe would put us to work every opportunity he had. We had to mow the lawn, separate the recyclables, and gather firewood. However, it was a small price to pay. There was plenty of fun to be had. We had lawn dart tournaments, Hacky Sack circles, Whiffle Ball games, and there was Geronimo. Geronimo was a 58-foot-high waterslide and the main attraction at Water Country in Portsmouth. The slide towered over the water park and dropped straight down at a ludicrous speed. It was the ultimate gut check for a bunch of teenage boys.

Joe traveled with his transgressions and became a folk hero of sorts in Rye. The beach across the street was a bit rocky and had a notoriously strong riptide. There were also no lifeguards, which made it more secluded than Jenness State Beach or Wallis Sands. Every now and then Joe would sneak across the street to smoke a joint. He would always bring Scooter, the Kellys' family dog who, oddly enough, shared many of Joe's personality traits. The two would turn up hours later at Petey's, the local pub in town.

One summer in the late 1980s, Rye hosted a blues festival. Luther "Guitar Junior" Johnson was the headliner, and other notable performers were on the bill.

"You're wasting the day away," Joe said, as he woke us up early the day of the festival and continued to bark marching orders in our direction. He always accused us of wasting the day away—It was his catch phrase.

He persuaded Shawn, Jay and me to head out on foot and get to the festival early, like he did in the 1960s. He swore to us that the concert grounds were only a mile down the road. Of course, this was before GPS and smartphones and the trek was more like ten miles.

Along the way, we met a guy in a wheelchair who was also headed to the festival. We decided to travel together and took turns pushing his wheelchair. We discussed life, girls, music, philosophy, and other heady topics on the journey. The more we talked, the more mysterious our travel companion became.

He revealed to us the events that led to his paralysis. He was at a party with friends and overindulged in illegal substances. In his intoxicated state, he decided to climb a gnarly tree. He slipped, fell to the ground and injured his spinal cord. He was confined to a wheelchair from that day forth. I found the revelation to be disconcerting. Our new acquaintance seemed to teeter on the edge of being sketchy and cool, if that's even possible.

Joe would love this guy, I thought. We arrived at the festival and entered the concert with our travel companion. He said he needed a drink and would be right back. We never saw him again.

Joe and Kathy drove to the festival and met us inside. Joe was on cloud nine and rocked out the entire afternoon. He had the opportunity to meet some of the musicians and he introduced us to Guitar Junior. Jay even posed for a photograph with him, which was pretty cool. I felt like I earned an associate degree in music that afternoon, and Joe was the dean of the blues.

In addition to the blues, Joe was also a connoisseur of fine hats. He had derby hats, Panama hats, safari hats, skimmer hats, straw hats, sun hats, fedoras, and more.

Joe would throw a party every Labor Day weekend. The parties varied in size from year to year. Some were small, just family and friends. Others were pretty epic and included a ton of people. One year he even had live music, and I lovingly coined the event "Bluestock." The celebrations always ended when Joe tossed his hat into the fire. It was a symbolic gesture, his way of bringing the party and another summer at the beach to an end. He would smile as the hat crackled and popped in the fire pit.

"Flanagan, this is God's country," he would always say.

15

REVENGE

We were back to the grind and on to the next job, which just happened to be Joe's attorney's house on the east side of Providence. The East Side is an affluent community and is home to Brown University, the Rhode Island School of Design, numerous private schools, and a variety of desirable shops and restaurants.

"Listen up, you two," Joe said. "I don't want to see any mistakes. I want perfection today. And for Chrissakes, buy some new pants. You look like a couple of bums."

Joe was always in a bad mood when he returned from Rye, and he proceeded to take it out on Jay and me. He made us set up the heavy staging not once but twice. We scraped and sanded the entire house with no help. There were no coffee breaks and he busted our balls throughout the day.

"Flanagan, get back to work." "Reddington, stop fucking around." "Work faster." "Work harder." He was relentless.

It was the end of the day and time to clean up. My hands were blistered and cramped. I grasped the hard wooden handle of the push broom and swept a pile of construction debris into the middle of a drop cloth. "Spirit in the Sky" by Norman Greenbaum came on the radio.

"Never been a sinner, I never sinned. I got a friend in Jesus. So you know that when I die, he's gonna set me up with the spirit in the sky."

Jay and I were perched on the top roof, two stories above Joe, who was bent over in the driveway attending to the paintbrushes. He dipped each brush into a bucket of paint thinner, then methodically wiped the bristles clean. His grumbling was insufferable.

"Blah, blah, blah, younger generation. Blah, blah, blah, back in my day."

I had reached my breaking point. The bee stings, the sunburn, the verbal abuse—teenage angst—whatever it was, something inside of me snapped. I stepped to the edge of the roof and stood high above Joe. His painter pants were hanging low, and I could see the crack of his hairy ass. I scooped up the heavy drop cloth loaded with paint chips, dust, caulk, nails, and other nasty material and held it over his head.

I looked at Jay, who looked at me and then at the loaded drop cloth pressed against my chest.

"Oh fuck," he whispered as he shook his head no.

His eyes pleaded with me not to do it. I turned and let go of the drop cloth. A dark shadow covered Joe. He looked up at the last second and I could see the whites of his eyes, but it was too late. The heavy drop cloth hit him dead on and buried him into the ground.

His white cotton painter's cap was knocked straight off his head. The ground filled with smoke, and Joe was pinned beneath the drop cloth. When the smoke cleared, I saw a hand penetrate through the canvas. A small edge of the tarp was lifted, and Joe's head poked through.

"FLANAGAN!"

He was beyond disheveled and roared with fury as he struggled to regain his balance and fight his way out of the drop cloth. I saw Jay out of the corner of my eye; he had tears streaming down his face.

"Redemption," I said under my breath.

"When I die and they lay me to rest. Gonna go to the place that's the best. When I lay me down to die, Goin' up to the spirit in the sky."

16

ROCKY POINT AMUSEMENT PARK

WARWICK, RHODE ISLAND

The celebration continued after the eulogy. My friend and local musician, Pat Baron, grabbed an acoustic guitar and dedicated one of his original songs to Joe. The song was entitled, "The Bucket is a Beautiful Place (sometimes)," and includes the lyrics, "Grand finale fireworks in McCoy. We'll miss you Mr. Kelly. You brought joy to those you loved." It was a fitting song and a wonderful way to wind down the wake.

I took a photo with Sherry and Jay's Uncle Kenny, our former fireworks supplier, and texted it to Jay. The celebration was a potluck and Jay, half-jokingly, asked if his mom had brought a "Potato Puff Surprise."

"Holy shit. I can't believe I almost forgot about that," I texted back.

I hadn't thought about a Potato Puff Surprise in decades and it made me smile. I drank one last beer, said goodbye, and left the Galway.

My dad took me to the airport the next day. It's an hour drive from Pawtucket to Boston and I made a mental note of the familiar landmarks along the way. There's the Rainbow

Swash, which is a natural gas tank located in Dorchester and is quite the spectacle on Interstate 93. The massive white tank is draped in a colorful rainbow. The design was created by Sister Mary Corita Kent and is the largest piece of artwork to be copyrighted in the world. Then there's the Dorchester Yacht Club that was founded in 1870. After that, there's the Boston Globe. The newspaper's iconic masthead always catches my eye. And finally, there is the Boston skyline. We entered the Ted Williams Tunnel and headed to my terminal.

I made it through security and boarded the plane. I had a window seat and gazed out over the city of Boston as the plane took off. I reflected on the funeral and the celebration of Joe's life at the Galway. We flew over the Narragansett Bay, which is comprised of numerous small islands and marine life, and plays an instrumental role in Rhode Island's ecosystem. However, when I think about the Narragansett Bay, I always think of Rocky Point, an amusement park that was located in Warwick, Rhode Island. I sat back in my chair, closed my eyes and thought about that summer day many years ago when the neighborhood spent the day at the park.

I rolled down the window as we approached the main entrance. The cool ocean breeze drifted through my parents' black station wagon. I caught a beam of light ricochet off the massive sign that was supported by concrete columns on both sides of the road. The crooked, red and blue letters that spelled, "R-O-C-K-Y P-O-I-N-T" radiated as the sun permeated across the whimsical marquee.

I started to hum the theme song as we passed through the entrance and entered the park.

"Come with your family. Come with your friends."

My humming turned into outright singing.

"That's the Rocky Point tradition 'cause it's summer time again."

Mike chimed in.

"Rocky Point, it's so exciting."

Then Timmy, Jay, John, and Pauly joined.

"Rocky Point, where you can come alive. Rocky Point, you're all invited to share our summer time. Rocky Point."

My parents parked the family wagon and we bolted to the ticket booth. Rocky Point was a Rhode Island institution. The park opened sometime in the 1840s and sat on the edge of the Narragansett Bay. Of course, there were rides, but there was also an Olympic-size saltwater swimming pool, an indoor and outdoor concert stage, and the world's largest shore dinner hall. The massive hall accommodated four thousand people and served a smorgasbord of New England delicacies, including clam cakes and chowder, steamers, lobster, corn, and fresh watermelon.

There were numerous visits every summer. There were field trips, birthday parties, family outings, you name it. Each visit was a visceral experience as vibrant screams of delight echoed across the park, and the sound of rides humming up and down the tracks sailed into the night. The smell of fried dough and cotton candy floated out of every concession stand and the sound of a Wurlitzer organ twisted its way around every corner. It was more than an amusement park; it was a complete sensory overload.

We purchased our tickets and strolled through the arched gateway. I glanced up and saw a young couple snuggled together in a lift chair. Their feet were crisscrossed and play-fully swung back and forth in midair about thirty feet above my head. The Skyliner was a ski lift that traveled across the park. It was a mellow ride, but gave you a bird's-eye view of the entire park.

"We should check out the Flume," Jay said.

"Let's do it," Mike said.

We walked over and stared up at the multistory drop. I was awestruck and felt a tiny hint of vertigo set in. The smell of chlorine hovered over the track as a group of riders passed us by and turned the corner. The Flume was Rocky Point's flagship attraction. It was a classic log ride that culminated with a sixty-foot plunge into a shallow pool that created quite the splashdown that soaked both passengers and spectators.

The slow and steady sound of the log ascending to the top of the ride grew louder and louder. Click clack, click clack, click clack. I shielded the sun with the palm of my hand and looked straight up. I saw the tip of the log. It inched forward and teetered on the edge of the lip for what felt like forever. Then it happened. The log plummeted down the steep track and crashed into the pool. We were hit with a tidal wave of ice-cold flume water, which prompted excitement and a few obscenities.

"Motherfucker," Pauly shouted.

"Goddamn that's cold," Mike said.

"Let's get in line," Jay said to the group.

The Flume was super popular and always had a long line, especially on hot summer days.

"Guys, I'm going to skip the Flume and check out some other rides. I'll catch up with you later," I said.

"That's cool," Jay said.

"Yeah, have fun," Mike said.

"I'll come with you, Tom" Pauly said.

Pauly stopped and bought a Coke at the concession stand, and then we made our way across the park. We passed a row of chance games. I never played these games, but I did enjoy watching the ones that actually required a certain degree of skill. There was a ring toss game called Ring Fling that I was always tempted to play. We stopped and watched a few people take a stab at Frog Bog. It was a fun game to watch.

Players had to launch a rubber frog onto a lily pad that floated on water and rotated clockwise on a continuous loop. The game required meticulous hand-eye coordination. There was Skee-Ball and of course, a variety of other sketchy carnival games.

We walked by the Musik Express. "Take on Me" by a-ha swirled around the ride.

"Shying away. I'll be coming for your love, okay? Take on me, take on me. Take me on, take me on. I'll be gone. In a day or two."

The Musik Express was a good opening act and a nice way to ease into the park. The ride was fast, but not too fast. The exterior featured psychedelic artwork of women, flowers, and butterflies. A dozen connected cars whipped around a tilted track, stopped, and then went backwards as distorted music roared from cheap speakers.

"Do you want to ride this?" I asked.

"What?" Pauly asked.

I leaned in and raised my voice. "Do you want to ride the Musik Express?"

"Fuck no," he said.

17

DING DONG DITCH

Paul Charpentier was the Sam Kinison of Agnes E. Little. By the age of nine, he had mastered profanity. He was a child prodigy and much to his parents' chagrin, four-letter words seemed to flow from deep within him. He also had a notoriously weak stomach.

We grew up in the 1980s. There were no smartphones. No Instagram, no Snapchat, and no Netflix. We created our own fun. We rode bikes and attempted death-defying jumps off of makeshift launch ramps made out of dilapidated plywood. We mastered inane sports like Jarts, Hacky Sack, and Nerf basketball. We ran up and down the neighborhood playing Manhunt and Tag until the streetlights came on. However, no game was more exhilarating or required more skill than Ding Dong Ditch. Ding Dong Ditch is the art of ringing a doorbell, then disappearing into the night before the unsuspecting victim can answer the door. Despite the simple premise, the prank took finesse. It took athleticism. It took balls.

The Blanchettes' house was nestled between Pauly's house and mine. Mr. Blanchette was a surly old man who unofficially policed the neighborhood. He felt compelled to lecture us every opportunity he had. It was his call to duty. God forbid your ball or frisbee landed in his yard. If it did, it was gone forever. He would even turn his garden hose on you if he heard you using language that he deemed inappropriate. Unfortunately, Pauly felt his frigid wrath on more than one occasion.

A couple weeks before our trip to Rocky Point, we were skateboarding in front of my house. As the sun began to set, Mike suggested that we play a round of Ding Dong Ditch. We were all veterans of the game and, as a unit, we functioned like a well-oiled machine. We all agreed, and Mike conducted a short reconnaissance to scope out a few prime spots. Our first target was a small Colonial located across the street from the church parking lot. Mike noted that it had an alleyway on the left side of the house and multiple escape routes. I volunteered to run point and lead the first ditch. I hid in the shadows behind the staircase and formulated my plan. The house had a bay window.

This complicates things.

The corner of the bay window faced the staircase, which provided an unobstructed view of the front door. The timing would be critical. I had to be fast and accurate. I analyzed the four steps up to the doorbell. I ran through a visualization exercise in my mind and envisioned myself ringing the bell as I evaporated into the night. One mistake and this whole thing could go sideways. Mike and Pauly lurked in the bushes across the street. Timmy camouflaged himself on the other side of the house. The others were scattered about.

A voice spoke from the shadows. "What are you waiting for? Do it."

My heart began to race. Adrenalin flowed through my body. I bolted towards the door. I skipped over the first step and stumbled up to the second. In one fluid motion, I steadied myself with my left hand, reached up with my right, rang the doorbell, and then hopped over the handrail. I ran away as fast as I could and didn't look back. I ran straight for my house and slid into the front yard. I ducked behind some bushes and kneeled in the dirt. Sweat poured down my face and my whole body tingled with electricity. I prayed that Mom didn't see me hiding in the bushes. Then I heard a stampede of sneakers gallop in my direction. The sound of the group's laughter was oddly reassuring. I slipped out of the bushes and played it cool.

"That was so amazing," Mike said as he gave me a high five.

"Did you see her face when she opened the door? It was classic," Timmy said.

"Okay, who's next?" I asked.

"Pauly should ring Blanchette's doorbell," Timmy said.

"Fuck that," Pauly said. "I ain't ringing that fucking bell."

Despite Pauly's objection, we had an ace up our sleeve. It was the same ace all teenage boys have. We busted his balls.

"C'mon Pauly."

"Don't be a chickenshit."

"Do it. Do it Pauly."

"What's the matter, you gonna cry?"

We were always coercing Pauly into some sort of trouble and it only took a few minutes to crack him. "Fine. I'll fucking do it," he said.

"Yes!" Timmy said, and the group cheered. This was the ditch to end them all and everyone wanted a front row seat. We hid in bushes and behind nearby trees. I ducked behind a car parked across the street. Pauly's hands were trembling by the time he reached the top step.

This is a suicide mission, I thought. There was no way this was going to end well, but heck, I certainly admired his courage. I mean, this took balls. He inched closer. A few giggles sounded from the bushes.

"Shush," someone whispered.

Pauly looked over his shoulder and threw a dirty look in our direction. He was on the cusp of neighborhood history. My hands were beginning to sweat just watching. The tension was palpable. He took a deep breath and then rang the doorbell.

"He did it. The crazy son of a bitch did it. He actually rang Blanchette's doorbell," I said.

However, the door didn't open and Blanchette was nowhere to be found. Not a single light was on and the house was completely silent. Something wasn't right.

Get out of there, Pauly. Abort the mission, I said to myself.

"Ring it again," Timmy barked.

Pauly hesitated for a moment, then rang the bell a second time. Once again, nothing happened. He turned and began to walk down the steps. All of a sudden, the door flew open.

"What do you want?" Blanchette said.

Pauly jumped. He was stunned and caught off guard. He turned and faced Blanchette. All he got out was, "Wanna buy a candy bar?"

Blanchette grunted and mumbled some expletives as he slammed the door in Pauly's face. We emerged from our hiding spots and ran over to the steps. We were drunk with delight.

"I can't believe it," Mike said.

"That was amazing," Timmy said.

"Want to buy a candy bar?" I asked.

We hovered around Pauly. I patted him on the back and the gang showered him with accolades. However, he seemed to be in a state of shock. He didn't say a word nor move a muscle. Then I caught a whiff of something rancid.

"Eww. What is that?" Mike asked.

A dark, brown liquid began to ooze down Pauly's leg.

"Oh my God," Timmy said. "He shit his pants."

Pauly just stood there with his hands on his stomach, completely befuddled.

18

FOAM

We walked past the Musik Express and headed in the direction of the Enterprise. Despite being overshadowed by newer rides such as the Free Fall and the Corkscrew roller coaster, the Enterprise was still a force to be reckoned with. We approached the ride as it was being lowered back into its base.

"There's no fucking way I'm getting on that ride," Pauly said.

"Roger that. Just hang out and watch. I won't be long."

It was a short line and I walked right up onto the platform and waited for the passengers to exit. The ride operator lifted the gate and I found an open gondola a few feet away. I jumped inside and strapped myself in. The seat was wet and there was a strange foam-like substance on the floor.

That's weird, I thought. *What the heck is that?*

The ride started harmless enough. It spun clockwise at a medium pace, not unlike a carousel. However, the ride took a turn for the worse and began to spin faster and faster, until I found myself in a centrifuge nightmare. The pressure in my chest began to mount. I could feel the blood whizzing through my veins, and I clenched the safety bar. Unfortunately, this was just the beginning. As the gravitational force reached its peak, the Enterprise lifted straight up and spun vertical like a Ferris wheel, spinning at a death-defying pace. I looked for Pauly down below and could only see a splatter of reds and yellows mixed with sky blue. I was on the verge of losing consciousness when the Enterprise finally began to slow down and descend back into its base.

"Thank God," I said.

The ride came to end, and I stepped out of the gondola. My legs felt like Jell-O and my Chuck Taylors were now covered in the strange substance.

"What do you wanna ride next?" Pauly asked.

"Something mellow," I said. "Let's go ride the House of Horrors."

The House of Horrors, or Castle of Terror, depending on how old you were, was a cross between a haunted house and the tunnel of love. The exterior of the two-story castle featured a Viking, horned helmet and all, standing over a speared dragon and surrounded by a stack of spired towers.

What the House of Horrors lacked in "horror," it certainly made up for in the relaxation department. Inside, the ride was dark and cool, and provided a nice change of pace from the more intense rides as well as an opportunity to get out of the sun for a few minutes. The walls of the castle were covered in ghoulish artwork illuminated with black lights and there was no shortage of campy props.

As the line inched closer, the smell of grease grew stronger. I looked over my shoulder and glanced up at the Sky Diver.

"We should ride that next," I said.

"Not a fucking shot." Pauly said.

We made it to the front of the line and the ride operator

waved Pauly and me forward. We walked through the turnstile and hopped into an old, weathered, fiberglass car that
had a faded portrait of Dracula painted on the front. The side
of the seat was covered in fossilized bubble gum that had
probably been there since the 1960s. The car took a sharp
right turn, crashed through a door, and entered what looked
like the dungeon of the castle.

"C'mon Pauly," I said. "Let's do it."

He stated his case and spun a perfect web of obscenities
to complement his argument.

"I don't give a flying fuck," he said.

"You're a goddamn bastard."

"You motherfucker."

"Go fuck yourself."

"What's the matter, Mommy won't let you ride the Sky
Diver?" I said.

"Are you crying?" I asked.

Our car toiled its way up to the second floor of the castle.
We slammed through the double doors and wrapped around
the balcony. It took a second for our eyes to adjust to the
sunlight, but we both caught a glimpse of the Sky Diver
lurking off in the distance. I was beginning to wear Pauly
down. I had him on the ropes and just needed to deliver a
knockout blow. I had to think fast.

"Afraid you'll crap your pants again?"

I don't know if Pauly felt the need to redeem himself
from the Ding Dong Ditch incident, but he had succumbed to
my relentless belittlement.

"Okay, okay. Enough. I'll go on the stupid ride, but under
one condition," Pauly said.

"What?" I asked.

"Don't spin the fucking car."

"Deal," I said.

We exited the House of Horrors and headed towards the Sky Diver. The Sky Diver was similar to a Ferris wheel in most regards, with two notable differences. First, the seats were fully enclosed, and second, the riders had the ability to spin the cars independently as the ride rotated.

Pauly and I walked up the ramp and waited by the turnstile for the ride operator's signal. The boarding process for the Sky Diver was slower and more thorough than other rides. Passengers had to be seated and properly secured one car at a time. The operator gestured to us. I rushed over and jumped into the car. Whereas, Pauly had the sense of urgency of a death row inmate heading to his execution.

"C'mon Pauly," I said.

"Hold your damn horses," he said.

Pauly poked his head into the car, examined the safety harness, then sat down on the seat, albeit reluctantly. The operator strapped us in and locked the door.

There's no turning back now.

There was a sudden jolt. This was followed by an ominous, almost metallic, grinding sound. Our car was lifted in the air. I looked at the steering wheel that was located at the center of the car, an arm's length from where Pauly and I sat, then I looked at Pauly.

"Don't you fucking dare," he said.

I couldn't help myself and lunged for the steering wheel. This in turn prompted a tsunami of profanity.

"You cocksucker motherfucker.

"You lie like a goddamn rug.

"Stop spinning the fucking car.

"You done fucked up."

Our car spun faster and faster as the Sky Diver continued to rotate. Inside the car, a battle royal had ensued as Pauly and I fought for control of the steering wheel. He twisted my arm with his left hand and threw a haymaker with his right that grazed the side of my head. I lost control of the steering wheel and the car began to spin out of control. All hell had broken loose as Pauly and I were tossed around the car like a couple of rag dolls. The relentless pounding obliviated my internal clock and any sense of time. Two minutes? Three minutes? Twenty minutes? I had no idea how long the ride lasted, but it finally began to slow down.

"Thank God," Pauly said.

"It's not over yet," I said.

"What the fuck does that mean?"

"Oh, you'll see," I said.

Pauly discovered that riders had to exit the Sky Diver one car at a time, just like the boarding process, and this meant the ride had to make one last full rotation. Our car reached the highest peak. The view of Narragansett Bay was stunning, and I decided the best way to appreciate this unique vantage point was to once again spin the car as fast as I could. Pauly begged me to stop. However, the more he pleaded, the faster I spun the car. The more he cursed, the more I laughed. It was pure torture.

The cursing and threats of physical violence had tapered off, and the car became eerily silent. I looked at Pauly and his face was white as a ghost. His neck tilted to the side, and then it happened. It was a violent explosion and I was instantly covered with the contents of his stomach. The car continued to spin out of control as I tried to shield myself from the vomit. I was pelted with every turn of the car and was even hit in the face with what appeared to be a small piece of a New York System wiener.

Did Pauly eat at the Right Spot?

In a cruel twist of fate, it was I who now cursed, and it was I who now pleaded for the ride to end.

"I told you not to spin the damn car," Pauly said.

I was horrified—on the verge of puking myself. I reached for the steering wheel and managed to steady the car as the ride came to an end. The operator walked over and opened the door. The inside of the car looked like a crime scene. However, the ride operator seemed surprisingly unfazed. He just whistled to one of his assistants who ran over with a white, plastic bucket.

"What the heck is that?" Pauly asked as we stepped out of the car.

The assistant handed the ride operator the bucket. It was filled with a sudsy detergent. The operator lifted the bucket up to his waist, tilted it sideways, and tossed the elixir into the car. I looked at the floor of the car, then down at my Chuck Taylors, and realized the origin of the strange foam that I encountered earlier on the Enterprise.

"So gross," I said as Pauly and I exited the ride with our heads hung in shame.

19

DADDY'S LITTLE EWOK

We began our approach towards Denver International Airport. Soaring across the Rocky Mountains and the Front Range is not for the faint of heart. However, it was a smooth descent and we landed safe and sound. I grabbed my carry-on bag from the overhead compartment and plotted my exit. I managed to circumvent a passenger who decided to head upstream to retrieve a bag located a few rows behind him, causing a traffic jam in the middle of the aisle. I thanked the pilot and the crew members, then exited the aircraft. It was a long flight. I needed to stretch my legs and get some fresh air, so I decided to walk to the long-term parking lot. I took out my phone and began to flip through my photos. There were photos of McCoy Stadium, The Galway, and Joe's funny Irish T-Shirt. I stopped at the photo of me, Sherry, and Jay's Uncle Kenny. I smiled and continued to search for the picture of the parking lot sign.

"Ah, section two," I said.

I found my car, jumped in, and headed back home. It's an hour drive straight up Interstate 25 from Denver to Fort Collins, and I used this time to think about the trip. Despite the circumstance, it felt good to visit the old neighborhood and catch up with friends and family. I thought about my adventures in home improvement. I thought about the eulogy and Kathy Kelly. I thought about Jenks Junior High School and battling bullies. I thought about my daughter, Marley, and how she had just started middle school. Then, I thought about when she was a baby and how fast time had passed.

I remembered the adorable onesie my wife Kathy and I bought her when she was six months old. It had a picture of Wicket on the front wearing his traditional brown, tattered cloak and holding his trademark spear. Under the image read the phrase, "Daddy's Little Ewok." It was a fond memory. Then a touch of sadness crept in, as I came to the realization that she was no longer my little Ewok. And all those nights we spent in a galaxy far, far away watching Luke Skywalker and Princess Leia battle Darth Vader and the Dark Side were coming to an end. Marley was growing up and about to embark on her own journey. One that would surely include arduous lockers and cafeteria hijinks. It was bittersweet.

I gave Kathy and Marley a big hug when I got home. We discussed the trip and I let them know that Joe's eulogy was well-received, and I did my best to make the Kellys proud.

"How was school?" I asked Marley.

"I have to share my locker with a classmate and the combination locks are really hard to open," she said. "I was almost late for a class."

Try being shoved into one, I thought to myself. But I just grinned and encouraged her to stick with it. Then the conversation turned to dinner.

"Dad, I'm hungry. What's for dinner?" Marley asked.

Deciding what to do for dinner always makes for a lively debate in my house. One that typically involves a painstaking exploration of available options followed by uncertainty, unrest, and finally, unmitigated compromise. However, this time was different.

"We're having the Potato Puff Surprise," I said.

Kathy looked puzzled and raised an eyebrow.

"What the heck is that?" Marley asked.

"Oh, you'll see," I said. "Jay's mother used to make it for us when we were kids."

The Potato Puff Surprise is a casserole that includes ground beef, gravy, shredded mozzarella cheese, and potato puffs. Lots of potato puffs. The secret ingredient, of course, is love. Now this might not sound appetizing to an actual grown adult, but to a kid it was the ultimate comfort food. The perfect delicacy on a cold winter day or after a rough week of school. It was one of my favorite childhood dishes, and something told me that Marley might enjoy it.

"I'm sorry about Mr. Kelly," Marley said.

"Me too," I said as I stepped into the kitchen to tackle the Potato Puff Surprise.

I never met anyone like Joe Kelly. He was a rebel and a scoundrel, a bluesman and a teacher, a husband and a father. God knows he wasn't perfect, but who is? He taught me how to sand and scrape, and how to prime and paint. But above all, he taught me to never waste a day.

EPILOGUE

Jay Reddington now lives in Austin, Texas and is one of my oldest and dearest friends. He came to visit over the Thanksgiving holiday. We had a wonderful time catching up, shopping in Old Town Fort Collins, and touring breweries. We had dinner, then watched an old movie from the 1980s that seemed far cooler when we were kids than it did now. Funny how that works.

After the movie, we exchanged war stories about working for the Blue Man. Jay worked for Joe longer than I did and shared a couple of doozies that I had never heard before. In Joe's quest to teach us responsibility and a potential trade that we could use in life, he could be a complete asshole. But there was another side to Joe. One that a lot of people may not know, but one I'd like to share.

Joe was always there. Jay's parents were divorced, and Joe was a surrogate father of sorts to him and John growing up. He also informally embraced that role with Pauly after Roger, Mike and Pauly's dad, was killed in an accident at work. Joe was more than happy to spend quality time with the neighborhood kids. He took us on vacation, on camping trips, and to baseball games when other parents didn't have the time or inclination. We were a bunch of misfits, but we were his misfits, and I have always admired that.

As the years rolled by, so did Joe. He grew to love the infamous "drop cloth" story. He had me tell it at parties, cookouts, and other celebrations. After a short battle with cancer, Joe passed on September 3rd 2017, Labor Day weekend. I promised him I would include the story in his eulogy and I did.

I learned a valuable lesson in craftsmanship that summer many years ago. Whenever I see something painted Battleship Gray, I think about scraping and the trials and tribulations of home improvement. I think about Luther "Guitar Junior" Johnson and the rich history of the blues. But most of all, I think of Joe Kelly.

AFTERWORD

Thank you for reading my book. I truly hope you enjoyed it. And I hope these stories unearthed a few, long forgotten memories from your childhood. If you have a story to share about growing up, drop me a line at tom@tflan.com. I'd love to hear it.

Also, visit tflan.com/surprise to see photos of Joe "Bluesy Ass" Kelly, Jay Reddington, Pauly Charpentier, and some of the other eclectic characters that make an appearance in this book. I may have even added a photo of Joe wearing his infamous Saint Patrick's Day T-Shirt.

ABOUT THE AUTHOR

Tom Flanagan was born and raised in Pawtucket, Rhode Island, home to the Industrial Revolution, the Pawtucket Red Sox, and the Division Street House of Pizza. He has a passion for telling stories about growing up, battling bullies, and dabbling in the dark art of home improvement.

Now residing in Fort Collins, Colorado with his wife Kathy and daughter Marley, Tom has finally decided to write down these stories and bring the eclectic cast of characters he grew up with to life.

 facebook.com/TomFlanaganAuthor

 twitter.com/tflan

instagram.com/tflan